Tale Of The Tape:
RIS JERICHO
Match Profile

Tale Of The Tape:
SHEAMUS
Match Profile

Tale Of The Tape:
DANIEL BRYAN
Match Profile

VS

P46

P70

P84

AM JOHNNY
Match Profile

Tale Of The Tape:
UNDERTAKER
Match Profile

Tale Of The Tape:
TRIPLE H
Match Profile

VS

# WWE Annual 2013 Contents

Welcome to the 2013 WWE annual! and congratulations on joining the Superstars of sports entertainment!

We've packed the pages with all the facts, figures, match stories, quizzes and more to make sure you're slammed with info and fun for the next twelve months!

What are you waiting for? Let's ring the bell and get this started!

Published 2012. Century Books Ltd.
Unit 1, Upside Station Building
Solsbro Road, Torquay, Devon
UK, TQ26FD

£7.99

NAME:              SANTINO MARELLA
HEIGHT:                      6'0"
WEIGHT:                   233 LBS
FROM:             CALABRIA, ITALY
SIGNATURE MOVE:   THE COBRA
CAREER HIGHLIGHTS:
INTERCONTINENTAL CHAMPION,
US CHAMPION, WWE TAG TEAM
CHAMPION

NAME:              KOFI KINGSTON
HEIGHT:                      6'0"
WEIGHT:                   212 LBS
FROM:       GHANA, WEST AFRICA
SIGNATURE MOVE:
TROUBLE IN PARADISE
CAREER HIGHLIGHTS:
INTERCONTINENTAL CHAMPION,
US CHAMPION, WWE TAG TEAM
CHAMPION, WORLD TAG TEAM
CHAMPION

NAME:              DAVID OTUNGA
HEIGHT:                      6'0"
WEIGHT:                   229 LBS
FROM: HOLLYWOOD, CALIFORNIA
CAREER HIGHLIGHTS:
WWE TAG TEAM CHAMPION

NAME:              JACK SWAGGER
'THE ALL-AMERICAN AMERICAN'
HEIGHT:                      6'7"
WEIGHT:                   260 LBS
FROM:          PERRY, OKLAHOMA
SIGNATURE MOVE:
ANKLE LOCK
CAREER HIGHLIGHTS:
WORLD HEAVYWEIGHT
CHAMPION, ECW CHAMPION,
US CHAMPION, MONEY IN THE
BANK WINNER

# ROSTER PROFILES

NAME: CHRIS JERICHO
HEIGHT: 6'0"
WEIGHT: 226 LBS
FROM: WINNIPEG, MANITOBA
SIGNATURE MOVE:
THE CODEBREAKER,
THE WALLS OF JERICHO
CAREER HIGHLIGHTS:
WWE CHAMPION,
WORLD HEAVYWEIGHT
CHAMPION, WCW CHAMPION,
& MANY MORE...

NAME: R-TRUTH
HEIGHT: 6'2"
WEIGHT: 220 LBS
FROM: CHARLOTTE,
NORTH CAROLINA
SIGNATURE MOVE:
LIE DETECTOR
CAREER HIGHLIGHTS:
US CHAMPION,
WWE TAG TEAM CHAMPION

NAME: MICHAEL McGILLICUTTY
HEIGHT: 6'3"
WEIGHT: 227 LBS
FROM: CHAMPLIN, MINNESOTA
CAREER HIGHLIGHTS:
WWE TAG TEAM CHAMPION

NAME: THE MIZ
HEIGHT: 6'2"
WEIGHT: 220 LBS
FROM: CLEVELAND, OHIO
SIGNATURE MOVE:
SKULL-CRUSHING FINALE
CAREER HIGHLIGHTS:
WWE CHAMPION, US CHAMPION,
WWE TAG TEAM CHAMPION,
UNIFIED TAG TEAM CHAMPION

NAME:                DOLPH ZIGGLER
HEIGHT:                      6'0"
WEIGHT:                   213 LBS
FROM:     HOLLYWOOD, FLORIDA
SIGNATURE MOVE: THE ZIG ZAG
CAREER HIGHLIGHTS:
WORLD HEAVYWEIGHT
CHAMPION,
INTERCONTINENTAL CHAMPION,
US CHAMPION

NAME:                 REY MYSTERIO
HEIGHT:                        5'6"
WEIGHT:                    175 LBS
FROM:   SAN DIEGO, CALIFORNIA
SIGNATURE MOVE:
619 AND WEST COAST POP
CAREER HIGHLIGHTS:
WWE CHAMPION, WORLD
HEAVYWEIGHT CHAMPION,
INTERCONTINENTAL CHAMPION,
WWE TAG TEAM CHAMPION,
& MANY MORE...

NAME:                BRODUS CLAY
                'THE FUNKASAURUS'
HEIGHT:                      6'7"
WEIGHT:                   375 LBS
FROM:            PLANET FUNK
SIGNATURE MOVE:
AH FUNK IT
CAREER HIGHLIGHTS:
WWE NXT RUNNER-UP

NAME:                          JTG
HEIGHT:                       6'2"
WEIGHT:                    232 LBS
FROM:      BROOKLYN, NEW YORK

# ROSTER PROFILES

**NAME:** KANE
'THE BIG RED MONSTER'
'THE DEVIL'S FAVORITE DEMON'
**HEIGHT:** 7'0"
**WEIGHT:** 323 LBS
**SIGNATURE MOVE:** CHOKESLAM
**CAREER HIGHLIGHTS:**
WWE CHAMPION, WORLD
HEAVYWEIGHT CHAMPION,
ECW CHAMPION,
INTERCONTINENTAL CHAMPION,
& MANY MORE...

**NAME:** TENSAI
**HEIGHT:** 6'7"
**WEIGHT:** 360 LBS
**FROM:** JAPAN
**SIGNATURE MOVE:**
THE CHOKEBOMB PIN
**CAREER HIGHLIGHTS:**
HAS RECENTLY DEFEATED
JOHN CENA, CM PUNK AND
R-TRUTH

**NAME:** MASON RYAN
**HEIGHT:** 6'5"
**WEIGHT:** 289 LBS
**FROM:** CARDIFF, WALES
**SIGNATURE MOVE:**
THE FULL NELSON SLAM

**NAME:** JERRY
"THE KING" LAWLER
**HEIGHT:** 6'0"
**WEIGHT:** 243 LBS
**FROM:** MEMPHIS, TENNESSEE
**SIGNATURE MOVE:**
PILEDRIVER, FLYING FISTDROP
**CAREER HIGHLIGHTS:**
AWA WORLD CHAMPION; WCCW
CHAMPION; MULTIPLE-TIME
REGIONAL CHAMPION,
& MANY MORE...

**NAME:** ZACK RYDER
**HEIGHT:** 6'2"
**WEIGHT:** 214 LBS
**FROM:** LONG ISLAND, NEW YORK
**SIGNATURE MOVE:**
ROUGH RYDER
**CAREER HIGHLIGHTS:**
US CHAMPIONSHIP, WORLD TAG
TEAM CHAMPION

**NAME:** ANTONIO CESARO
**HEIGHT:** 6'5"
**WEIGHT:** 232 LBS
**FROM:** LUCERNE, SWITZERLAND
**SIGNATURE MOVE:**
VERY EUROPEAN UPPERCUT

**NAME:** CAMACHO
**HEIGHT:** 6'2
**WEIGHT:** 230 LBS
**FROM:** JUAREZ, MEXICO

**NAME:** DAMIEN SANDOW
**HEIGHT:** 6'4"
**WEIGHT:** 243 LBS
**FROM:** NORTH OXFORD,
MASSACHUSETTS
**SIGNATURE MOVE:**
THE ILLUMINATION

# ROSTER PROFILES

NAME: BOOKER T
HEIGHT: 6'3"
WEIGHT: 256 LBS
FROM: HOUSTON, TEXAS
SIGNATURE MOVE:
SCISSOR KICK
CAREER HIGHLIGHTS:
WORLD HEAVYWEIGHT CHAMPION,
WCW CHAMPION, WORLD TAG
TEAM CHAMPION, WCW WORLD
TAG TEAM CHAMPION,
& MANY MORE...

NAME: DARREN YOUNG
HEIGHT: 6'1"
WEIGHT: 239 LBS
FROM: MIAMI, FLORIDA
SIGNATURE MOVE:
THE GUT CHECK

NAME: DREW MCINTYRE
HEIGHT: 6'5"
WEIGHT: 254 LBS
FROM: AYRE, SCOTLAND
SIGNATURE MOVE:
FUTURE SHOCK
CAREER HIGHLIGHTS:
INTERCONTINENTAL CHAMPION,
WWE TAG TEAM CHAMPION

NAME: ALBERTO DEL RIO
HEIGHT: 6'5"
WEIGHT: 239 LBS
FROM: SAN LUIS POTOSI, MEXICO
SIGNATURE MOVE:
CROSS ARMBREAKER
CAREER HIGHLIGHTS:
WWE CHAMPION, ROYAL
RUMBLE WINNER (2011),
RAW MONEY IN THE BANK
WINNER (2011)

NAME: CHRISTIAN
HEIGHT: 6'1"
WEIGHT: 212 LBS
FROM: TORONTO, CANADA
SIGNATURE MOVE: KILLSWITCH
CAREER HIGHLIGHTS:
WORLD HEAVYWEIGHT
CHAMPION,
ECW CHAMPION,
INTERCONTINENTAL CHAMPION,
WORLD TAG TEAM CHAMPION,
& MANY MORE...

NAME: THE GREAT KHALI
HEIGHT: 7'1"
WEIGHT: 347 LBS
FROM: INDIA
SIGNATURE MOVE:
PUNJABI PLUNGE;
KHALI VISE GRIP
CAREER HIGHLIGHTS:
WORLD HEAVYWEIGHT
CHAMPION

NAME: HEATH SLATER
HEIGHT: 6'2"
WEIGHT: 216 LBS
FROM: PINEVILLE,
WEST VIRGINIA
CAREER HIGHLIGHTS:
WWE TAG TEAM CHAMPION

NAME: HUNICO
HEIGHT: 5'10"
WEIGHT: 205 LBS
FROM: MEXICO CITY, MEXICO

# ROSTER PROFILES

NAME: RANDY ORTON
HEIGHT: 6'5"
WEIGHT: 235 LBS
FROM: ST. LOUIS, MISSOURI
SIGNATURE MOVE: RKO
CAREER HIGHLIGHTS:
WWE CHAMPION, WORLD
HEAVYWEIGHT CHAMPION,
INTERCONTINENTAL CHAMPION,
WORLD TAG TEAM CHAMPION,
2009 ROYAL RUMBLE MATCH
WINNER

NAME: MARK HENRY
HEIGHT: 6'4"
WEIGHT: 412 LBS
FROM: SILSBEE, TEXAS
SIGNATURE MOVE:
WORLD'S STRONGEST SLAM
CAREER HIGHLIGHTS:
WORLD HEAVYWEIGHT CHAMPION,
ECW CHAMPION;
EUROPEAN CHAMPION

NAME: JUSTIN GABRIEL
HEIGHT: 6'1"
WEIGHT: 213 LBS
FROM: CAPE TOWN,
SOUTH AFRICA
SIGNATURE MOVE:
450 SPLASH
CAREER HIGHLIGHTS:
WWE TAG TEAM CHAMPION

NAME: TYSON KIDD
HEIGHT: 5'10"
WEIGHT: 195 LBS
FROM: CALGARY,
ALBERTA, CANADA
CAREER HIGHLIGHTS:
UNIFIED TAG TEAM CHAMPION,
WWE TAG TEAM CHAMPION

# DIVAS

**NAME:** LAYLA
**FROM:** MIAMI, FLORIDA
**CAREER HIGHLIGHTS:**
DIVA'S CHAMPION, WINNER OF
THE 2006 $250,000 DIVA
SEARCH, WOMEN'S CHAMPION

**NAME:** AJ
**HEIGHT:** 5'3"
**FROM:** UNION CITY, NEW JERSEY
**SIGNATURE MOVE:**
SHINING WIZARD

**NAME:** AKSANA
**HEIGHT:** 5'6"
**FROM:** ALYTUS, LITHUANIA

**NAME:** BETH PHOENIX
'THE GLAMAZON'
**HEIGHT:** 5'7"
**FROM:** BUFFALO, NY
**SIGNATURE MOVE:**
THE GLAM SLAM
**CAREER HIGHLIGHTS:**
DIVAS CHAMPION, WOMEN'S
CHAMPION

# ROSTER PROFILES

NAME: VICKIE GUERRERO
HEIGHT: 5'4"
FROM: EL PASO, TEXAS
SIGNATURE MOVE:
COUGAR SPLASH

NAME: KELLY KELLY
HEIGHT: 5'5"
FROM: JACKSONVILLE, FLORIDA
CAREER HIGHLIGHTS:
DIVAS CHAMPION

NAME: ALICIA FOX
HEIGHT: 5'9"
FROM: PONTE VERDA BEACH,
FLORIDA
SIGNATURE MOVE:
SCISSOR KICK
CAREER HIGHLIGHTS:
DIVAS CHAMPION

NAME: EVE
HEIGHT: 5'8"
FROM: DENVER, COLORADO
CAREER HIGHLIGHTS:
DIVAS CHAMPION, 2007 WWE
DIVA SEARCH WINNER

# Tale Of The Tape:
# JOHN CENA
## Match Profile

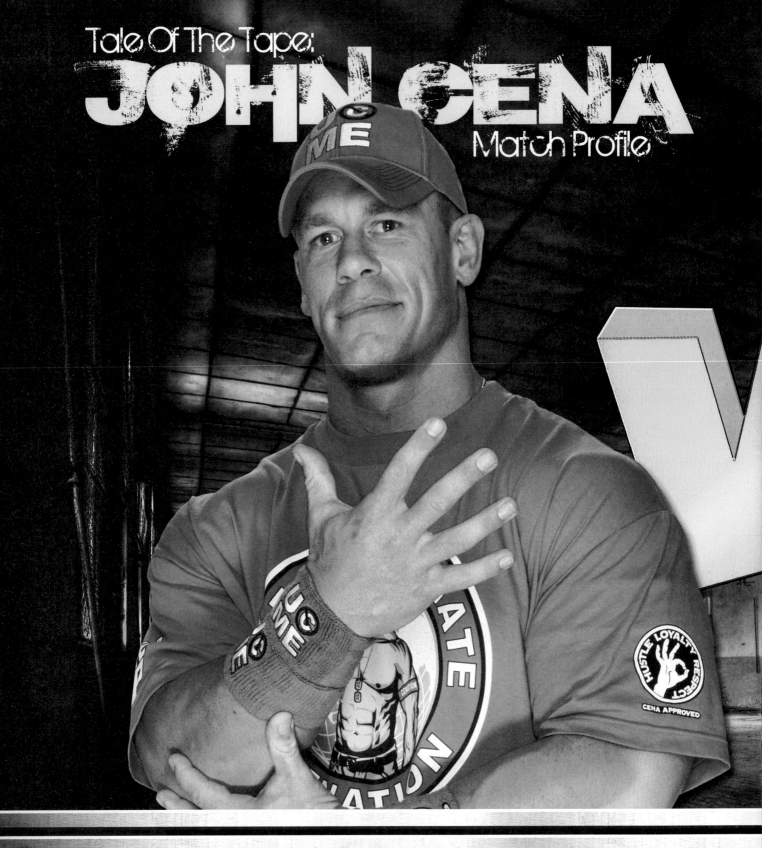

**HEIGHT:** 6'1"
**WEIGHT:** 251 LBS
**FROM:** WEST NEWBURY, MASSACHUSETTS
**SIGNATURE MOVE:** ATTITUDE ADJUSTMENT, STF
**CAREER HIGHLIGHTS:** WWE CHAMPION, WORLD HEAVYWEIGHT CHAMPION, US CHAMPION, WORLD TAG TEAM CHAMPION, WWE TAG TEAM CHAMPION, 2008 ROYAL RUMBLE WINNER, 2010 SUPERSTAR OF THE YEAR SLAMMY AWARD WINNER

## Did you know?

o Cena's debut music album, 'You Can't See Me', was an instant hit. The album reached number 15 on the Billboard 200 chart and number three in the rap charts. His classic track 'My Time Is Now' is still a fan favourite.

o Aside from wrestling, John Cena also has a busy career starring in action movies. He has starred in four WWE Studios feature films.

o John is a huge sports fan and supports a variety of teams in different sports, including the *Tampa Bay Rays*, an American Major League Baseball team.

o John also holds some pretty impressive records outside of the ring. He has granted more than 300 wishes to the seriously ill children at the Make-A-Wish-Foundation.

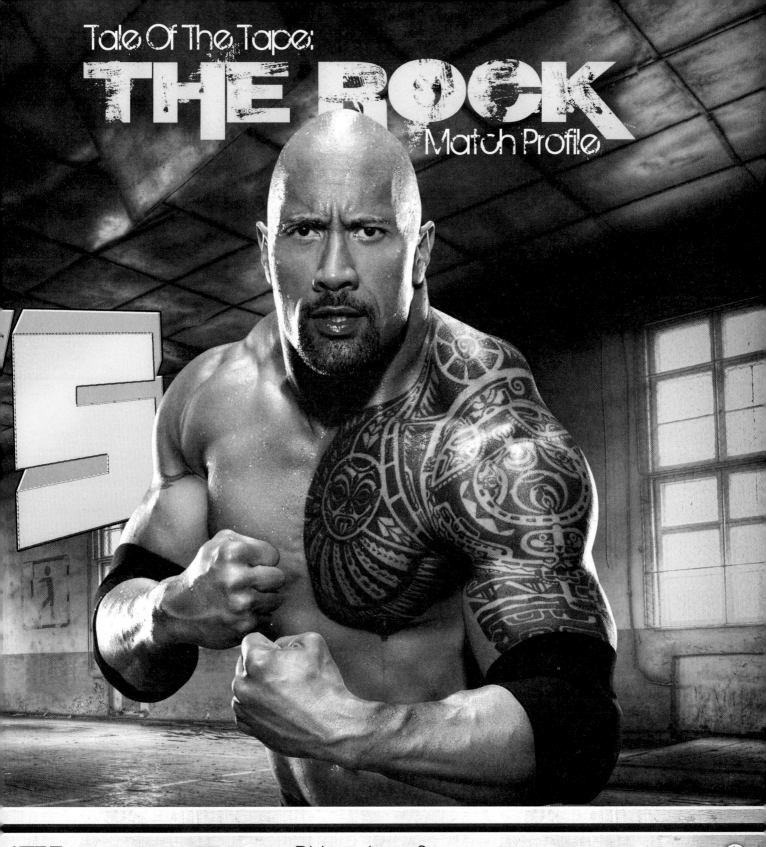

# Tale Of The Tape:
# THE ROCK
## Match Profile

| | |
|---|---|
| **HEIGHT:** | 6'5" |
| **WEIGHT:** | 260 LBS |
| **FROM:** | MIAMI, FLORIDA |

**SIGNATURE MOVE:**
ROCK BOTTOM, PEOPLE'S ELBOW

**CAREER HIGHLIGHTS:**
WWE CHAMPIONSHIP,
INTERCONTINENTAL CHAMPION,
WORLD TAG TEAM CHAMPION,
ROYAL RUMBLE WINNER (2000),
WCW CHAMPION

## Did you know?

○ The Rock ia a third generation Superstar. His father, Rocky Johnson and grandfather High Chief Peter Maivia both made their livings inside the ring.

○ His debut novel The Rock Says made it to the top of the New York Times' best-seller lists!

○ His fellow Superstars voted The Rock the award for 'best talker' in the company's history.

○ The Rock has also dipped his toes into the music biz. In 2000, he was featured on Wycelf Jean's song 'It Doesn't Matter'.

"Here he is folks, Massachusetts' finest - John Cena! A quick salute to the *WrestleMania* fans and he's ready to go!"

"...and the Cenation is in a hurry to get this thing started! He's sprinting to the ring!"

"It's The Rock! Over a year in the making, the fans in attendance are about to witness the most-hyped match-up the WWE has ever had!"

"The most-famous elbow in sports! The Rock shows off his most-famous, and dangerous, weapon the People's Elbow. But will he get the chance to land it on Cena tonight?"

"After months of tension and trash talking, these two are finally about to get their hands on each other! The referee moves them to a neutral corner, the bell rings and its go-time in a Once In A Lifetime match-up!"

"The Rock looks ready and Cena means business! This truly is going to be a match for the ages, never has a fight been better named – Once In A Lifetime!"

"The Rock has Cena locked in a headlock and he's not going anywhere! These two Superstars have set a ferocious pace in these opening exchanges."

"Rock's using every fibre in his body to put pressure on the Cena's neck."

"It's a hip-toss! Rock seems to be getting the better of Cena in these first few minutes. But can he maintain this incredible pace for the whole match?"

"Woah! That's a huge shoulder barge, I bet they could feel that right at the back of the stadium. Rock's really laying it on Cena here!"

"But wait, Cena has him! He's caught Rock in a huge bear hug and is squeezing the life out of him. You can see the pain etched on Rock's face."

"Rock's going for a ride! Cena's turned the bear hug into a brutal belly-to-belly suplex!"

"What's this?! Rock is back on his feet, he seems impervious to pain right now!"

"Cena isn't letting that deter him though. He comes off the ropes and lands a huge flying shoulder barge to put Rock back on the canvas."

"And Cena has no intention of letting Rock get back up. He's landed a devastating right hand off the top rope. No one can take this sort of punishment!"

"He's going for it! Cena has Rock ready for an Attitude Adjustment! Surely it's just a matter of time now, no one recovers from this devastating move."

"Oh he lands it. He goes for the cover and it's One, Two.... Rock's kicked out! How is he recovering from this?!"

"But as The Rock's trying to recover, Cena has climbed to the top rope again and is coming down with the biggest leg drop we've ever seen!"

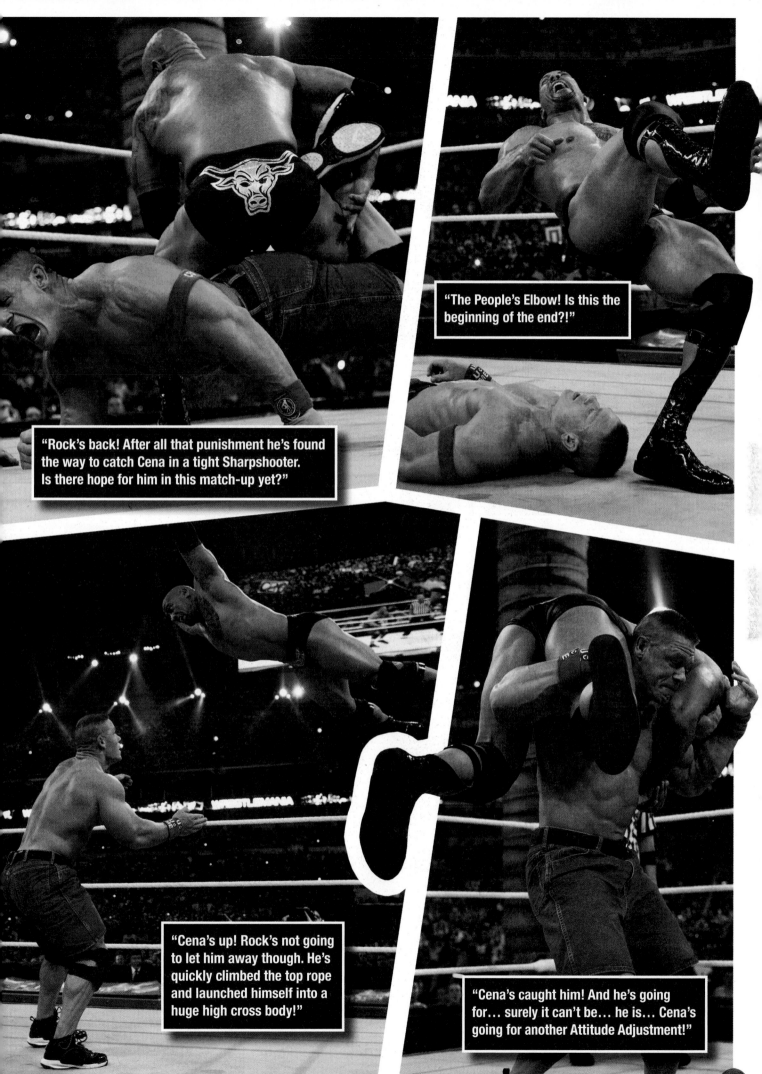

"Rock's back! After all that punishment he's found the way to catch Cena in a tight Sharpshooter. Is there hope for him in this match-up yet?"

"The People's Elbow! Is this the beginning of the end?!"

"Cena's up! Rock's not going to let him away though. He's quickly climbed the top rope and launched himself into a huge high cross body!"

"Cena's caught him! And he's going for... surely it can't be... he is... Cena's going for another Attitude Adjustment!"

"Boom! Cena landed it! Rock's back was crashed into the canvas with incredible force.

But instead of the cover, he's going for, I don't believe it, a People's Elbow!"

"Rock countered it and landed a brutal Rock Bottom!"

"Rock goes for the cover. One, Two, Three! He's won it! The crowd are going wild, no one can believe what they have just seen."

"Ladies and gentleman, you're winner by pinfall. The Rock!"

"Cena looks devastated but he should be incredibly proud of himself this evening. That was one of the most incredible matches in the history of WWE and sports entertainment!"

"The Rock, the Once In A Lifetime winner of a Once In A Lifetime match!"

# THE HEAVYWEIGHT WWE QUIZ
## PART ONE
# HALL OF FAME

RE YOU A WWE SUPERSTAR IN WAITING? TO RUB SHOULDERS WITH THE BEST YOU HAVE TO KNOW ABOUT THE ATHLETES HO MADE THE SPORT THE INCREDIBLE SPECTACLE THAT IT S TODAY. GET READY TO TEST YOUR KNOWLEDGE ON SOME OF SPORT ENTERTAINMENT'S GREATEST LEGENDS...

**1. BRET HART WAS KNOWN AS THE EXCELLENCE OF EXECUTION THANKS TO HIS PERFECT TECHNIQUE. BEFORE EACH MATCH HE WOULD GIVE A PRESENT TO ONE LUCKY FAN, WHAT WAS IT?**

A. A KISS

B. HIS MIRRORED GLASSES

C. A SIGNED PICTURE

**2. HULK HOGAN AND MACHO MAN RANDY SAVAGE MADE A NAME FOR THEMSELVES IN THE 1980S WORKING TOGETHER AS A TAG TEAM. WHAT WERE THEY CALLED?**

A. THE MEGA POWERS

B. THE POWER MONGERS

C. THE SUPER POWERS

**3. CURRENT WWE SUPERSTAR CODY RHODES HAS AN EQUALLY FAMOUS FATHER. CAN YOU NAME HIM?**

A. GOLDUST

B. GARY RHODES

C. DUSTY RHODES

**4. WHO WAS YOKOZUNA'S MANAGER WHEN THE GIANT SUMO PLAYER BECAME THE YOUNGEST SUPERSTAR TO WIN THE WWE CHAMPIONSHIP?**

A. BOBBY HEENAN

B. JIMMY HART

C. MR FUJI

**5. HOW MANY FEET TALL DID ANDRE THE GIANT STAND?**

a. 7'4"
b. 7'1"
c. 7'3"

**6. ONE OF THE MOST-SHOCKING MOMENTS IN WWE HISTORY CAME WHEN JAKE THE SNAKE ROBERTS'S PET SNAKE DAMIAN WAS CRUSHED UNDERNEATH A HEAVY RIVAL. WHO WAS JAKE'S ENEMY?**

a. TYPHOON
b. EARTHQUAKE
c. KING KONG BUNDY

**7. STONE COLD STEVE BUSTIN WAS A HUGE FAN FAVOURITE DURING HIS TIME WITH THE WWE. FANS OFTEN USED TO HOLD UP POSTERS REFERRING TO A BIBLICAL SIGN OFTEN SEEN AT SPORTING EVENTS. WHICH PASSAGE WAS IT?**

a. JOHN 3:16
b. JOHN 16:3
c. JAMES 3:16

**8. WHO IS THIS FORMER WWE CHAMPION?**

a. THE ULTIMATE FIGHTER
b. THE TOTAL OPPONENT
c. THE ULTIMATE WARRIOR

**9. WHAT YEAR WAS SHAWN MICHAELS INDUCTED INTO THE WWE HALL OF FAME?**

a. 2010
b. 2011
c. 2012

**10. WHOSE FINISHING MOVE WAS THE PAINFUL COBRA CLUTCH?**

a. THE IRON SHEIK
b. ZEUS
c. SERGEANT SLAUGHTER

JOHN CENA

28

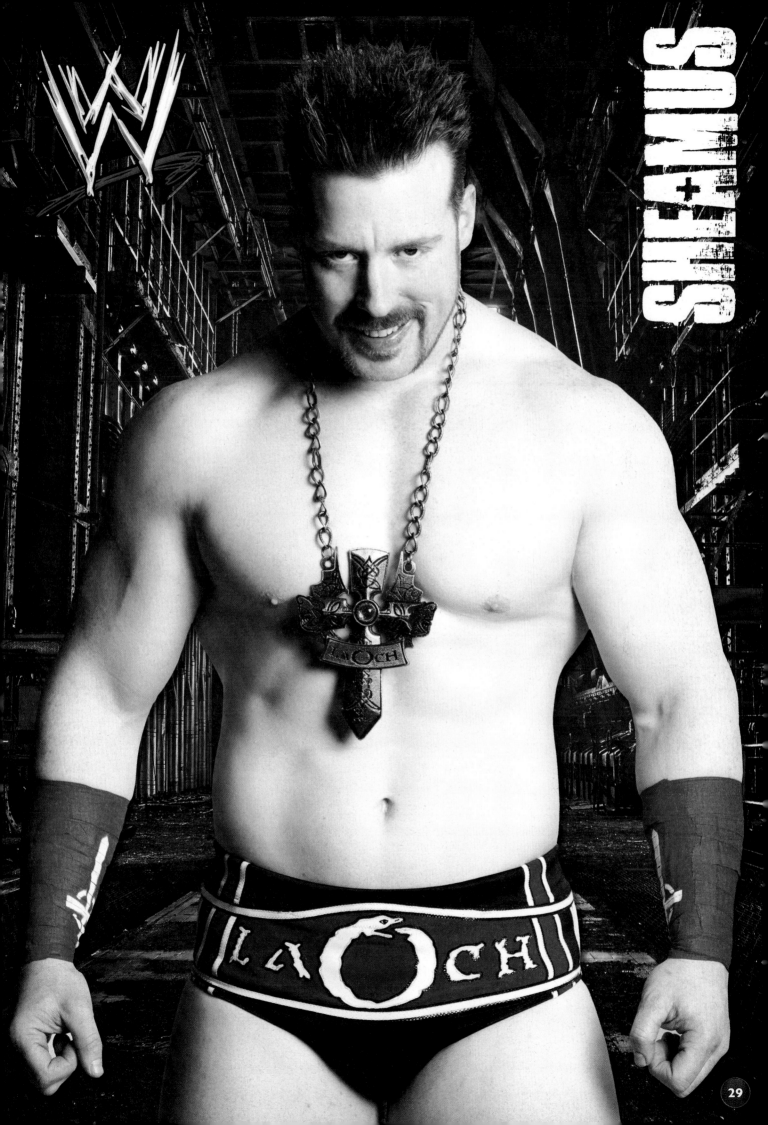

SHEAMUS

29

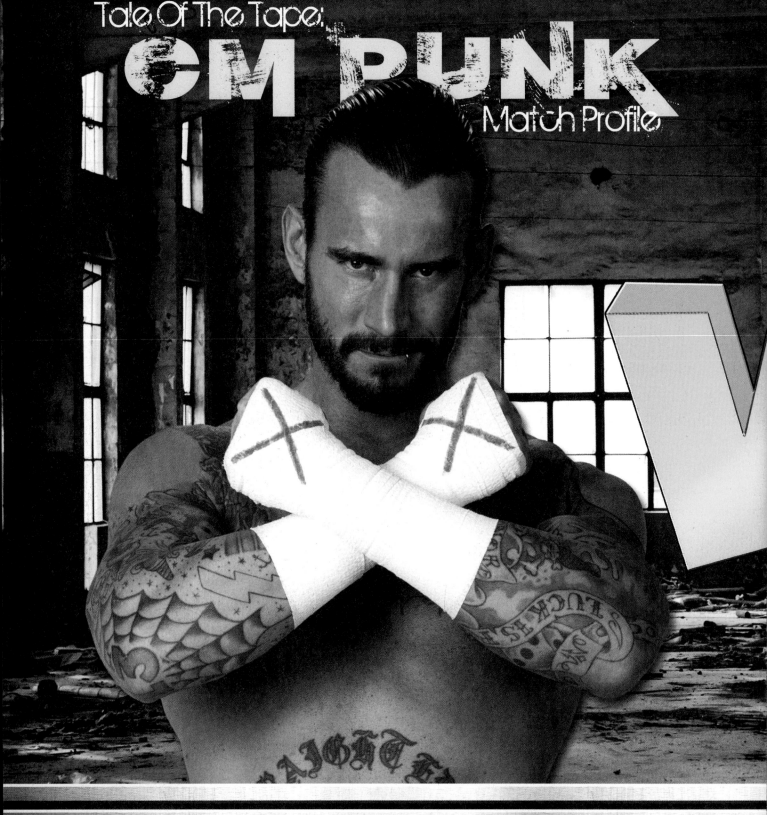

# Tale Of The Tape:
# CM PUNK
## Match Profile

**HEIGHT:** 6'2"
**WEIGHT:** 218 LBS
**FROM:** CHICAGO, ILLINOIS
**SIGNATURE MOVE:**
GTS (GO TO SLEEP),
ANACONDA VISE
**CAREER HIGHLIGHTS:**
WWE CHAMPION, WORLD
HEAVYWEIGHT CHAMPION,
ECW CHAMPION, WORLD TAG
TEAM CHAMPION,
INTERCONTINENTAL CHAMPION,
RAW COMMENTATOR

## Did you know?

o Punk lists Hall of Famer Rowdy Roddy Piper as his biggest inspiration and the reason he became a wrestler.

o As well as a champion Superstar, Punk is a committed and vocal supporter of the Straight Edge movement – a subculture that rejects the use of drugs, alcohol and a dependency lifestyle.

o Many theories exist regarding the origin of CM Punk's name. However, Punk has denied any connection with an early tag team he joined in his early years called the Chick Magnets, insisting that the initials have no meaning at all.

o Punk has many tattoos, one of the most prominent being a Pepsi logo on his left shoulder. Whenever he is asked why he chose to have it done, Punk answers 'I like Pepsi!'

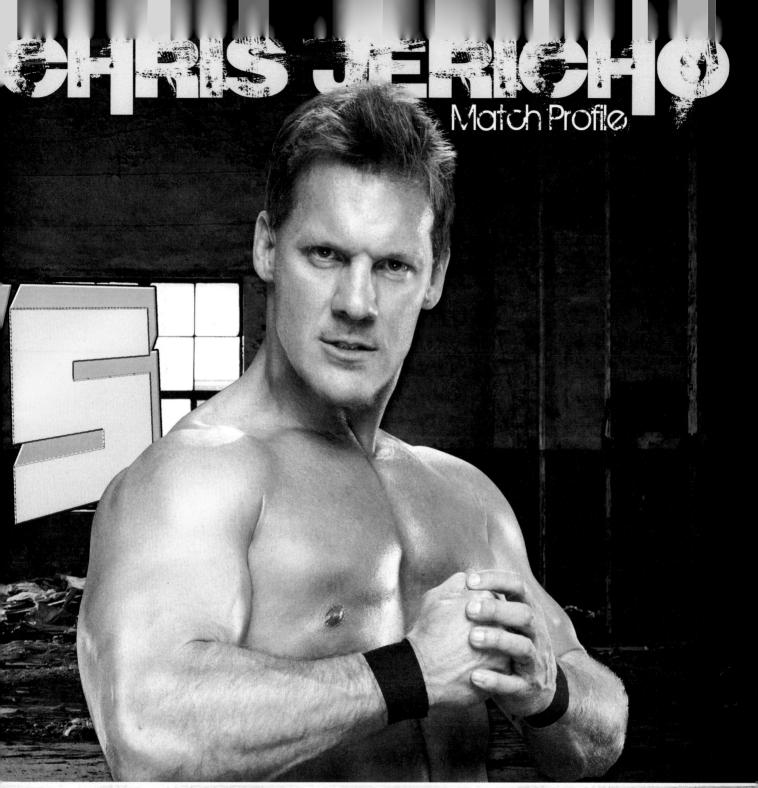

# CHRIS JERICHO
## Match Profile

**HEIGHT:** 6'0"
**WEIGHT:** 226 LBS
**FROM:** WINNIPEG, MANITOBA
**SIGNATURE MOVE:**
THE CODEBREAKER,
WALLS OF JERICHO
**CAREER HIGHLIGHTS:**
WWE CHAMPION; WORLD
HEAVYWEIGHT CHAMPION;
WCW CHAMPION; INTERCONTINENTAL
CHAMPION; EUROPEAN CHAMPION;
HARDCORE CHAMPION;
WORLD TAG TEAM CHAMPION; ECW TV
CHAMPION & MANY MORE...

## Did you know?

- The Ayatollah of Rock N Rolla holds the record for most Intercontinental Championship reigns. Nine so far and counting!

- Jericho's metal band Fozzy have released four studio albums and one live recording since forming in 1999.

- Chris' fast feet haven't only helped him out in the ring. He was a contestant on Dancing with the Stars in 2011, where he made it to the fifth round.

- Y2J is credited by many as being the innovator of Money in the Bank Ladder Match, a WWE tradition that has led to nearly 10 World Title reigns.

"Here comes the Ayatollah of Rock N Rolla! Jericho knows that if he can get Punk to lose his temper tonight and get disqualified, he'll win the WWE Championship. What plans does he have in store?"

"Jericho has taunted the champion in the build-up to this match-up. He's attacked Punk, interfered in his matches and made it personal by insulting members of his family and even vowed to make CM Punk break his straight edge philosophy. It's now time for him to back up it all up!"

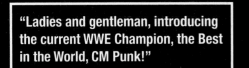

"Ladies and gentleman, introducing the current WWE Champion, the Best in the World, CM Punk!"

"Look at the focus on Punk's face. He's never looked as serious or ready for a match-up in his WWE career!"

"The crowd are going crazy for Punk. But despite all the noise, he hasn't taken his eyes off Jericho once!"

"That's what it's all about folks, the WWE Championship! Both these Superstars have laid claim to being the Best in the World, tonight we get to find out who it really is!"

"Punk goes straight to work and lands a series of viscous elbows on a downed Chris Jericho."

"The action is ferocious! Punk is on the top rope and it looks like he's going to try and land something from high above the arena floor!"

"Punk hits the high-cross body! He must've been 15 feet above the ground there – that hurts just to look at!"

"Punk has a steel chair in the ring. Jericho is goading the champion to use it but if he does it will mean an instant DQ and Jericho automatically being named WWE Champion."

"Punk didn't use the chair but the distraction was enough to switch the momentum in this match to Jericho's favour and the challenger quickly lands a side-suplex from the apron and straight on to the arena floor."

"All of Jericho's insults about Punk's father and sister have fired the champion up though and he's soon on top again. He's mounted the turn buckle and is going for a huge elbow drop from the top!"

"Jericho's going for the Walls of Jericho! Will he have the power to complete the move?"

"...But Jericho just gets his knees up in time and has got the upper-hand again. He ties the champ up and lands a Codebreaker!"

"He's showboating! Punk is laid out on the canvas, why isn't Jericho going for the cover? Will he live to regret this?"

"It's another Walls of Jericho and this time he has it sunk in deep. It must be only a matter of time before Punk taps and Jericho is named the new champion!"

"The pain is written across Punk's face but he seems to be drawing strength from the crowd's cheers. Maybe this match isn't over just yet?"

"Punks out and is laying the hurt on Jericho! He's on the top rope again and goes for a huge splash from the top rope!"

"Get ready to go for a ride Jericho! Punk has the challenger on his shoulders and is looking to slam him down to the canvas."

"Jericho locks up a third Walls of Jericho, Punk can't take this sort of punishment much longer."

"But wait! Punk has reversed the move and turned it into an Anaconda Vise and got the tap!"

"Punk is showing the crowd how much tonight's brutal match-up meant to him. Jericho made it personal and paid the price."

"CM Punk is STILL the WWE Champion! And after this epic match has won the right to call himself the Best in the World."

"Chris pushed the champion to the limit but in the end Punk's will was just to big. There was no way he was losing the championship tonight. Whatever it took, he was leaving with the title!"

# Spot The Difference

LOOK AT THESE KNOCK-OUT PICTURES OF CM PUNK AND CHRIS JERICHO'S INCREDIBLE MATCH-UP AT WRESTLEMANIA XXVIII. OUR CRACK TEAM OF COMPUTER WHIZZES HAVE MADE TEN TINY CHANGES TO EACH SET OF PICTURES. CAN YOU SPOT THEM ALL?

# NAME THAT SUPERSTAR

How well do you know the WWE Superstars? Could you still recognise them even if you only caught a glimpse of their awesome frames? Let's find out! Fill in the blanks to correctly name all ten Superstars below.

1. _ _ _ _ _   _ _ _ _ _ _ _ _

2. _ _ _ _ _ _   _ _ _ _ _ _

3. _ _ _ _ _ _ _   _ _ _ _

4. _ _ _ _ _ _ _   _ _ _ _ _ _ _

5. _ _ _ _ _ _ _

6. _ - _ _ _ _ _

7. _ _ _ _ _ _ _

8. _ _ _ _ _   _ _ _ _ _

9. _ _ _ _ _ _   _ _ _ _ _

WE'VE FOUND OUT IF YOU HAVE BEEN PAYING ATTENTION TO THE HISTORY OF THE WWE, BUT HOW'S YOUR KNOWLEDGE OF THE COMPANY AS A WHOLE? GRAB A PEN, FOCUS YOUR MIND AND PUT YOUR WWE KNOWLEDGE TO THE TEST...

**1. MONDAY NIGHTS ARE THE TRADITIONAL HOME FOR WHICH WWE SHOW?**

A. MONDAY NIGHT RAW
B. BEATDOWN MONDAY
C. START THE WEEK WITH SMACKDOWN

**2. HOW MANY DIFFERENT SINGLES TITLES ARE UP FOR GRABS IN THE WWE?**

A. 4
B. 5
C. 6

**3. WHAT IS TRIPLE H'S OFFICIAL JOB TITLE?**

A. CHIEF EXECUTIVE
B. VINCE MCMAHON'S PERSONAL ASSISTANT
C. CHIEF OPERATING OFFICER

**4. WHAT IS THE NAME OF WWE'S MASSIVE SUMMER MUST-SEE?**

A. SUMMERSLAM
B. SUMMERSMASH
C. SUMMERSMACK

**5. WHERE ARE THE WWE'S HEADQUARTERS BASED?**

A. STAMFORD, CONNECTICUT

B. LAS VEGAS, NEVADA

C. NEW YORK, NEW YORK

**6. COLOUR COMMENTATOR MICHAEL COLE CALLS HIMSELF 'THE VOICE OF WWE'. WHO DID HE REPLACE AS COMMENTATOR ON MONDAY NIGHT RAW?**

A. JIM ROSS

B. JOSH MATHEWS

C. JERRY LAWLER

**7. WHO IS KNOWN FOR THE CATCH PHRASE, "YOU'RE FIRED!"?**

A. GORILLA MONSOON

B. TRIPLE H

C. MR MCMAHON

**8. TEDDY LONG IS KNOWN AS THE FORMER LONG-TIME GENERAL MANAGER OF WHICH WWE EVENT?**

A. SMACKDOWN

B. RAW

C. SURVIVOR SERIES

**9. WHAT IS WWE NXT?**

A. A SEARCH FOR THE NEXT SUPERSTAR

B. THE CRUISERWEIGHT DIVISION

C. THE EUROPEAN FIGHT LEAGUE

**10. WHO IS JIM ROSS?**

A. A DECORATED REFEREE

B. THE FIRST EVER WWE CHAMPION

C. A LEGENDARY COMMENTATOR

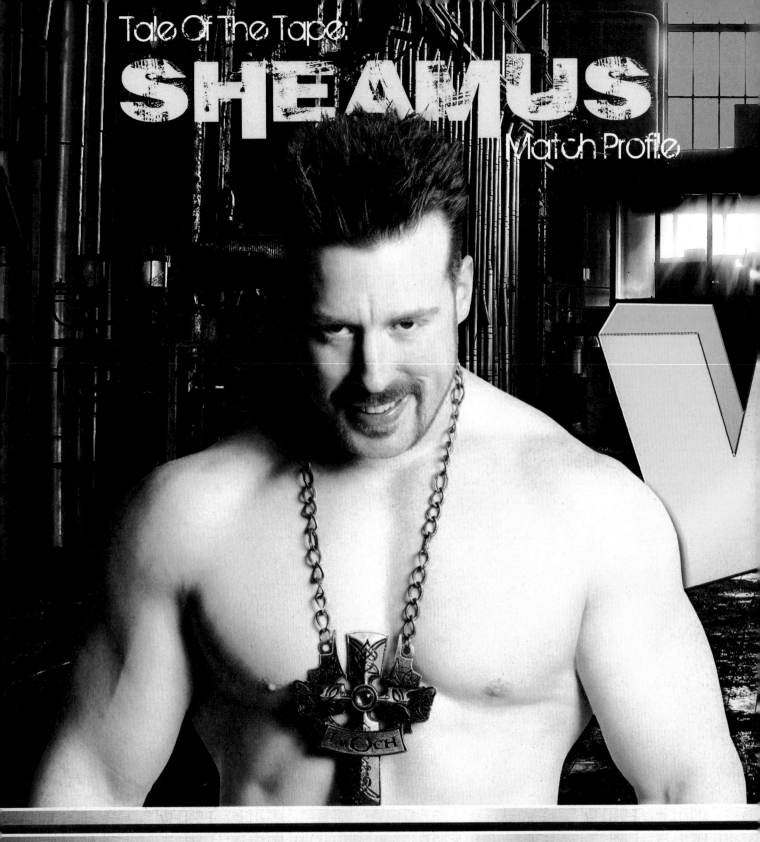

# Tale Of The Tape:
# SHEAMUS
## Match Profile

**HEIGHT:** 6'4"
**WEIGHT:** 267 LBS
**FROM:** DUBLIN, IRELAND
**SIGNATURE MOVE:**
BROGUE KICK, IRISH CURSE, HIGH CROSS
**CAREER HIGHLIGHTS:**
WWE CHAMPION, WORLD HEAVYWEIGHT CHAMPION, US CHAMPION, 2010 KING OF THE RING, 2012 ROYAL RUMBLE MATCH WINNER

## Did you know?

○ During his school years, Sheamus sang in the Palestrina Choir at home in Dublin and even appeared on several television programmes.

○ Before becoming a full-time wrestler, Sheamus worked as a personal security guard for U2!

○ Sheamus was given advice on how to become a Superstar from Hall of Famer Bret Hart.

○ Sheamus made his WWE debut back in 2006 when Raw visited Manchester.

# Tale Of The Tape:
# DANIEL BRYAN
## Match Profile

HEIGHT: 5'10"
WEIGHT: 210 LBS
FROM: ABERDEEN, WASHINGTON
SIGNATURE MOVE:
"YES!" LOCK
CAREER HIGHLIGHTS:
WORLD HEAVYWEIGHT CHAMPION,
US CHAMPION, 2011 SMACKDOWN
MONEY IN THE BANK WINNER

## Did you know?

- Daniel Bryan is arguably the best trained Superstar in the WWE! For ten years he worked closely on his technique with the Heartbreak Kid himself, Shawn Michaels.

- Outside the ring Bryan is a committed vegan, turning to the diet when he had a liver infection. Since making the change he was awarded a Libby Award from PETA for being the 'Most Animal-Friendly Athlete'.

- Wrestling has taken Daniel all over the world. Before becoming a WWE Superstar he spent time out of the spotlight working on his skills in Japan, the UK and Canada.

"What an incredible scene here at *WrestleMania*. The perfect setting for a match-up to decide who should hold the World Heavyweight Championship!"

"First to the ring, the challenger. All the way from Dublin, Ireland, Sheamus! The crowd are going crazy, it's easy to tell who they're backing tonight!"

"Champion Bryan better look out tonight. That's 6'4" of bad intentions making his way to the ring!"

"Sheamus has promised to use his Celtic Cross and his fans from all over the world to give him the strength to win the title tonight. He has a reputation for being a fast starter, let's see if he can get off to the right start this evening."

"We are ready for the arrival of the champion, Daniel Bryan!"

"The crowd are booing Bryan with every step he takes to the ring! Have we ever heard such a bad reaction to World Heavyweight Champion?"

"It's like Bryan can't hear the boos though! He seems completely unaffected by the crowd's noise. Confidence has never been a problem for this Superstar!"

48

"Ever the gentleman, Bryan waits for his girlfriend AJ to open the ropes for him so he can climb into the ring! Who said chivalry was dead!?"

"Ladies and gentleman, your World Heavyweight Champion. Daniel Bryan!"

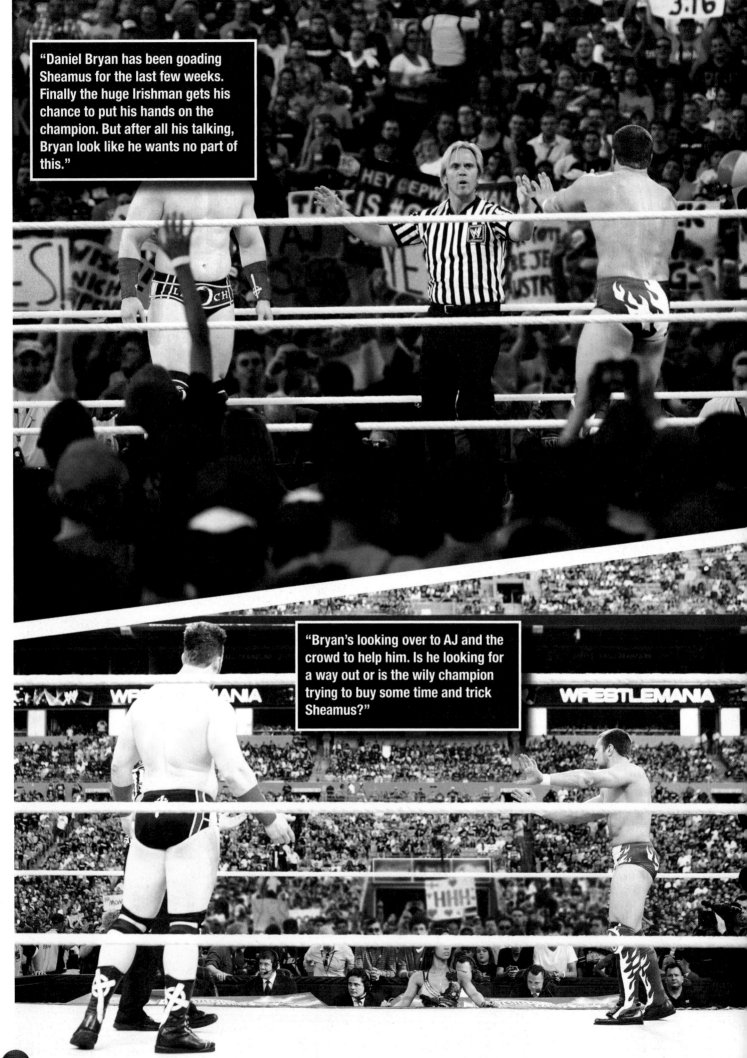

"Daniel Bryan has been goading Sheamus for the last few weeks. Finally the huge Irishman gets his chance to put his hands on the champion. But after all his talking, Bryan look like he wants no part of this."

"Bryan's looking over to AJ and the crowd to help him. Is he looking for a way out or is the wily champion trying to buy some time and trick Sheamus?"

"But there's no tricking Sheamus! He's in a hurry to get this under way, desperate to stop Bryan talking and wants to lift the Championship gold. Just seconds after the bell rings he's gone straight for his finisher and landed a thunderous Brogue Kick to the chin of the champion!"

"Bryan's down. Even the ref can't believe how quickly this is happening. Sheamus is going for the pin and, One, Two, Three – we have a new World Heavyweight Champion!"

"Sheamus has done it! He warned Bryan before the match that he could expect a quick and painful fight and that's exactly what happened. We have a new World Heavyweight Champion!"

"Daniel Bryan and AJ are in a state of shock! They can't believe what's just happened. In one of the fastest matches in WrestleMania history, he's been defeated and lost his title!"

"Ladies and gentleman the winner and new World Heavyweight Champion. Sheamus!"

"It took Sheamus just 18 seconds to record the win and secure the title! What a perfect performance. A blink-and-you've-missed-it title success. He couldn't of dreamed for a better night than this!"

In the ring or on the mic, there's no missing a WWE Superstar! There are a host of great competitors hiding in the grid below. You'll need to look hard to find the 18 names in the word square – the words could be running in any direction.

| T | R | I | P | L | E | H | W | R | Y | D | E | R | F | G |
|---|---|---|---|---|---|---|---|---|---|---|---|---|---|---|
| R | A | A | H | K | E | W | V | S | G | Q | R | E | F | H |
| U | N | D | E | R | T | A | K | E | R | D | E | D | G | E |
| E | D | F | C | E | N | A | E | E | V | A | P | A | C | A |
| W | Y | S | O | B | Q | C | B | A | A | K | I | N | L | R |
| Q | O | X | D | B | D | W | J | G | L | N | C | I | Q | T |
| L | R | E | Y | M | Y | S | T | E | R | I | O | E | L | B |
| T | T | D | R | W | V | X | G | N | B | F | G | L | Q | R |
| R | O | I | H | U | N | I | C | O | T | Z | D | B | H | E |
| E | N | B | O | U | D | S | W | V | S | H | K | R | B | A |
| K | R | D | D | P | S | H | E | A | M | U | S | Y | K | K |
| O | Q | D | E | A | V | N | G | S | E | G | A | A | V | K |
| O | K | D | S | V | A | H | I | O | S | W | V | N | R | I |
| B | R | O | C | K | L | E | S | N | A | R | V | D | B | D |
| Y | I | H | O | R | N | S | W | O | G | G | L | E | R | L |

**BOOKER T • UNDERTAKER • TRIPLE H • EDGE
REY MYSTERIO • DANIEL BRYAN • HEARTBREAK KID
HORNSWOGGLE • BROCK LESNAR • KANE • SHEAMUS
EPICO • CODY RHODES • CENA • RANDY ORTON • JTG**

# Colossal Crossword

THIS BRAINBUSTER WILL WORK YOUR WWE KNOWLEDGE TO THE MAX! USE THE CLUES BELOW TO FILL THE ANSWERS IN THE GRID.

## ACROSS:
1. The WWE's Chairman, CEO and also a former WWE champ.
5. Former American football star _____ O'Neill. Made his name in WWE NXT.
7. The event that 30 men enter, but only one man wins.
10. A former tag team champion that could get you in a Million Dollar Dream.
11. Winner of the 2007 WWE Diva Search.
12. Shawn Michaels' shortened alias.
14. The WWE event where you are most likely to see a cage match.
15. Superstar Abraham Washington is sometimes known as All World, but most of the time people call him__.
16. Rey, WWE's master of the high-risk manoeuvre.

## DOWN:
2. If you're not competing in SmackDown, you've got to be in _ _ _
3. Multiple former-champion who puts opponents away with the Skull-Crushing Finale.
4. The niece of former WWE Legend Bret Hart.
6. WWE Diva Layla's surname.
8. The biggest athlete in professional sports.
9. The Superstar that teamed up with Kofi Kingston to form Air Boom.
10. Legend, former-champ and now a movie star, Dwayne Johnson.
12. WWE Legend Bret The____ Man Hart.
13. Seven foot one of Indian bad intentions, The Great _ _ _ _ _.

55

# Tale Of The Tape:
# BIG SHOW
## Match Profile

| | |
|---|---|
| **HEIGHT:** | **7'0"** |
| **WEIGHT:** | **441 LBS** |
| **FROM:** | **TAMPA, FLORIDA** |

**SIGNATURE MOVE:**
CHOKESLAM, KNOCKOUT PUNCH

**CAREER HIGHLIGHTS:**
WWE CHAMPION, WCW CHAMPION,
ECW WORLD CHAMPION, WORLD
TAG TEAM CHAMPION,
WWE HARDCORE CHAMPION,
US CHAMPION, WWE TAG TEAM
CHAMPION, INTERCONTINENTAL
CHAMPION

## Did you know?

o Big Show has the largest feet in the WWE. How big? Enormous, size 22 EEEEE to be exact – over 15 inches long and eight inches wide!

o Big Show is a six-time world champion. He's won the WCW World Heavyweight Championship twice, the WWE Championship twice, the ECW Championship once and the World Heavyweight Championship once, making him the first person ever to hold all four championships.

o First appearing in the WWE as an enforcer for company head honcho Mr McMahon, Big Show debuted by throwing Stone Cold Steve Austin into the wall of a steel cage, breaking the cage.

o Outside of WWE, Big Show is also a successful actor.

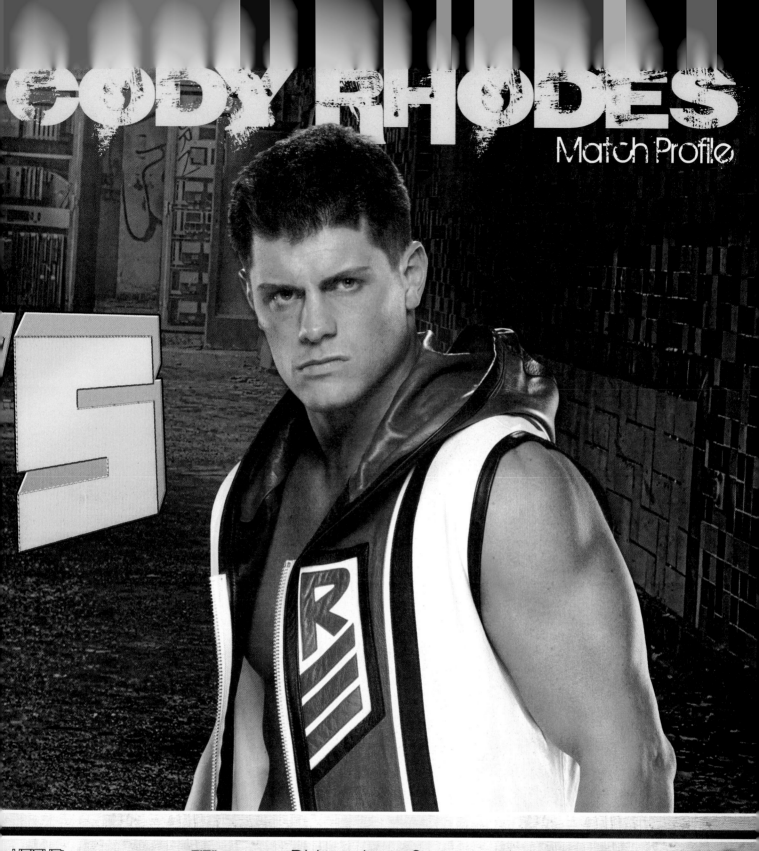

# CODY RHODES

## Match Profile

**HEIGHT:** 6'2"
**WEIGHT:** 215 LBS
**FROM:** MARIETTA, GEORGIA
**SIGNATURE MOVE:**
THE CROSS RHODES
**CAREER HIGHLIGHTS:**
INTERCONTINENTAL CHAMPION,
WORLD TAG TEAM CHAMPION,
WWE TAG TEAM CHAMPION

## Did you know?

○ Sports entertainment is built into Cody's DNA. His father is WWE legend "The American Dream" Dusty Rhodes, while his half brother is former WWE star Dustin Rhodes, better known as Goldust.

○ After being voted the Most Handsome Superstar by a poll of Divas for WWE.com, Cody decided to add to his stage name. And the word he chose? Dashing!

○ In 2009, Rhodes, along with Chris Jericho and John Cena became the faces of Gillette razors.

○ Cody is a huge comic book fan and admits his distinctive in-ring gear is inspired by his love of comics including the X-Men characters Cyclops and Omega Red.

"…And here comes the Intercontinental champ, Cody Rhodes! Never short of self-belief, and has gonna need every ounce of it tonight. He has a truly huge challenge in front of him if he wants to keep hold of the gold!"

"He certainly seems to be lapping up the attention of the *WrestleMania* fans here in Miami. But is his mind on the job?"

"But wait, what's this?!"

"Wow, Cody got serious in a second! Big Show's on his way and it's time to get down to business."

"Did Show get even bigger?! He looks huge tonight and, ominously for Rhodes, like he can't wait to get his hands on the young Superstar!"

"After weeks of publics jibes from Rhodes about his performances in previous *WrestleManias* Big Show looks like he's going to enjoy every second of this!"

"Rhodes better be ready to back up his words…"

"…But where has Cody gone? The Big Show is in the ring but there's no sign of the Intercontinental champ!"

"Bad news for the Intercontinental champ, he couldn't run all night! Show has his hands on Rhodes and is landing some huge open hand slaps."

"The crowd are enjoying this almost as much as the big man as they count every strike. It's not scientific, but Big Show is getting the job done! It looks like he's taking out weeks of frustration."

"Rhodes is trying to turn the tide and goes for a huge dropkick. If he can get Show to the mat he evens up the size difference. But wait, Show is impervious! He's brushed Cody aside like he was swatting a fly!"

"Cody's not ready to give up his title that quickly, he's landed a huge disaster kick. Will this slow Show down?"

"...Cody connects! The huge Miami crowd are glued to this scrap. Surely, this kick will give the champ the chance to inflict some damage of his own."

"Oh no, it only seems to have annoyed Big Show! He's gone straight back to landing some huge strikes. Cody better do something soon or it's going to be all over."

"Incredible! Against the flow of action, Cody has hit Show with a second disaster kick and this has finally registered on the big man, who has fallen to the canvas in a heap!"

"Now it's time for Cody to land some significant strikes of his own. Show is trying to make his way back to his feet, but after working so hard to get him down, Cody isn't letting go anywhere and unloads with a series of huge shots."

"Great strategy from the champ, he's softening Show up with a footlock. Can he tie up the other leg and turn it into a figure-four?"

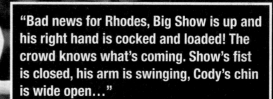

"Bad news for Rhodes, Big Show is up and his right hand is cocked and loaded! The crowd knows what's coming. Show's fist is closed, his arm is swinging, Cody's chin is wide open…"

"…and it lands! Big Show has landed a huge WMD on the champ. Goodnight! Are we about to see the title change hands?"

"Rhodes is down! All that remains is for Big Show to go for the cover and wait for the ref to count 'One, two, three!'"

"Ladies and gentleman, the NEW Intercontinental champion. Big Show!"

"Show can't believe what just happened. After winning every other title in the game, he finally has his hands on the Intercontinental gold!"

"What a night for the big man. He entered the ring hoping to settle a score and leaves with a strap!"

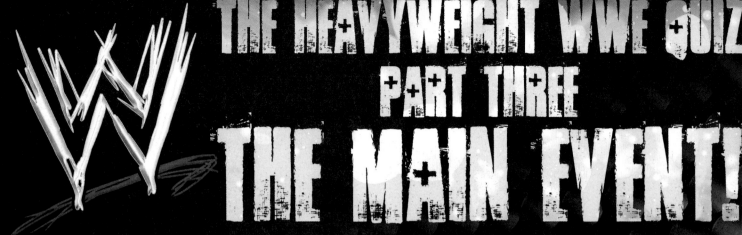

YOU'RE READY FOR THE BIGGEST STAGE OF ALL, ALMOST! YOUR NEXT CHALLENGE IS TO ANSWER SOME TOUGH QUESTIONS ABOUT SOME OF THE BIGGEST MATCHES IN WWE HISTORY. EYES DOWN FOR A PERFECT TEN...

**1. WHO DID JOHN CENA BEAT TO WIN THE WWE CHAMPIONSHIP AT *WRESTLEMANIA XXVI*?**

A. SHAWN MICHAELS

B. BATISTA

C. KANE

**2. UNDERTAKER MANAGED TO BEAT HBK AT *WRESTLEMANIA XXV* BY LANDING A LATE TOMBSTONE. HOW DID MANAGE IT?**

A. HE CAUGHT MICHAELS'

B. MOONSAULT MR MCMAHON INTERVENED AND DISTRACTED HBK

C. HE CAUGHT MICHAELS' HIGH-CROSS BODY

**3. HOW MANY SECONDS DID SHEAMUS NEED TO BEAT DANIEL BRYAN AT *WRESTLEMANIA XXVIII*?**

A. 16

B. 17

C. 18

**4. LEGENDS HULK HOGAN AND THE ULTIMATE WARRIOR MET AT *WRESTLEMANIA VI*. WHAT WAS SPECIAL ABOUT THEIR MATCH?**

A. IT WAS THE FIRST TIME A TITLE-FOR TITLE MATCH HAPPENED IN THE WWE

B. THEY WERE TAG TEAM PARTNERS

C. IT WAS IN A STEEL CAGE

## 5. WHO DID BRET HART FACE AT WRESTLEMANIA XXVI?

A. JIM NIEDHART
B. STU HART
C. MR MCMAHON

## 6. CM PUNK FOUGHT TWO SUPERSTARS AT SUMMERSLAM 2011. THE FIRST WAS JOHN CENA, WHO WAS THE SECOND?

A. TRIPLE H
B. ALBERTO DEL RIO
C. KOFI KINGSTON

## 7. WHO WON THE 2012 ROYAL RUMBLE?

A. CHRIS JERICHO
B. CHRISTIAN
C. SHEAMUS

## 8. EDGE, REY MYSTERIO, MIKE KNOX, KANE AND JOHN CENA ENTERED THE ELIMINATION CHAMBER AT NO WAY OUT IN 2009. WHO CLAIMED THE VICTORY?

A. EDGE
B. MIKE KNOX
C. KANE

## 9. CHRISTIAN WON A 20-MAN BATTLE ROYAL TO FACE THE INTERCONTINENTAL CHAMPION AT OVER THE LIMIT IN 2012. WHO DID HE FACE?

A. CODY RHODES
B. SANTINO MARELLA
C. BRODUS CLAY

## 10. BIG SHOW DEFEATED MARK HENRY AT SURVIVOR SERIES 2011. HOW DID HE WIN?

A. DISQUALIFICATION
B. PINFALL
C. COUNT-OUT

# Tale Of The Tape:
# TEAM TEDDY
## Match Profile

**HEIGHT:** 5'7"
**WEIGHT:** 173 LBS
**FROM:** ATLANTA, GEORGIA
**CAREER HIGHLIGHTS:** GENERAL MANAGER OF SMACKDOWN AND ECW

## Did you know?

o Teddy has worked his way up to the top in sports entertainment. His first job was running errands and sweeping the ring between matches in local shows.

o Long has been with WWE since 1999, but spent the first three years working for the company as a referee before making the switch to management.

o During his career he has managed 17 superstars and 4 tag teams.

o His first action after landing the job of SmackDown General manager was to hand Kurt Angle a $5,000 fine for appearing without his wrestling gear, much to the delight of the WWE fans!

# Tale Of The Tape:
# TEAM JOHNNY
## Match Profile

**HEIGHT:** 6'3"
**WEIGHT:** 225 LBS
**FROM:**
PHILADELPHIA, PENNSYLVANIA
**CAREER HIGHLIGHTS:**
WWE'S EXECUTIVE VICE PRESIDENT OF TALENT RELATIONS, GENERAL MANAGER OF RAW, GENERAL MANAGER OF SMACKDOWN

## Did you know?

○ Sports entertainment is in John's blood. His older brother is WWE Hall of Famer Animal from the Legion of Doom.

○ After a long spell working behind the scenes, Laurinaitis first became known to fans when he was described as a "glad-handing, nonsensical, yes-man" by CM Punk!

○ While he has tried to give himself the nicknames Mr Excitement and Big Johnny, the only one moniker that has really stuck was the one coined by Punk - Clown Shoes!

○ Before being fired by Mr McMahon, Laurinaitis received three Attitude Adjustments from the Cenation leader!

"Not short on self-belief it's The Miz!"

"Hold on to your hats, here comes a smorgasboard of Superstars for this special 12-man tag team match. First to the ring is Laurinaitis' Team Johnny, led by the fearsome Mark Henry"

"The last man to join Team Johnny after an injury (caused by the hands of CM Punk) ruled Christian off the card, it's Drew McIntyre!"

"Followed into the ring by his tag-team partner, Dolph Ziggler!"

"The last member of the team to make his way to the ring is the team's dangerous captain, David Otunga!"

"And finally, the man they're all fighting for John Laurinaitis"

"Next is tag-team specialist Jack Swagger!"

"Ladies and gentleman, we give you Team Johnny!"

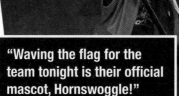

"Leading the way, supporting and introducing Team Teddy is one half of the Bella Twins, Nikki Bella!"

"Waving the flag for the team tonight is their official mascot, Hornswoggle!"

"Wow, Kofi Kingston looks fired up and ready to go tonight!"

"I hope they've strengthened the ring tonight, The Great Khali looks even bigger than normal!"

"R-Truth looks focused and ready tonight!"

"...and her comes Zack Ryder who's being accompanied to the ring by the delicious Diva Eve!"

"Here's Team Teddy's top man, captain Santino Marella!"

"And head-to-toe in blue, it's the man himself Teddy Long!"

"Team Teddy's cleared the ring! Team Johnny are nowhere to be found! In the Centre of the ring Hornswoggle waves the Team Teddy flag, letting everyone they're here to take charge!"

71

"Finally the action starts. And straight away R-Truth and Kofi Kingston are taking it to Dolph Ziggler. They've teamed up and landed a brutal double suplex. That shook the whole arena!"

"But Ziggler's recovered! He's landed a huge drop kick on Truth and doing some arena shaking himself!"

"This match-up is back and forth. The momentum has switched again and now Truth is way above the ring dropping a monstrous leg on a prone Ziggler."

"But The Miz made the tag and now it's the turn of Mark Henry and he's trying to turn the tide into Team Johnny's favour. A devastating slam on Booker T is a good way to start!"

"Now it's Booker T's turn to put the hurt on Team Johnny. He's landed a huge right hand straight into The Miz's kisser!"

"The captain's in the ring. Never be fooled by Marella's goofiness though, this Superstar knows how to wrestle! He's caught Miz in a fast and powerful hip toss that slams Team Johnny's man into the canvas."

"Marella's leading by example here. He's flattened The Miz and is now dropping a huge forearm on him for good measure!"

"Wait, is that? It is! Marella's unleashed the Cobra on Miz. One lethal strike and he's down. That was venomous!"

"Boom, The Miz hit the deck hard! That's gotta be it for Team Johnny. The rest of the team are tied up outside the ring, all it needs now is for someone to cover Miz and let the ref count to three!"

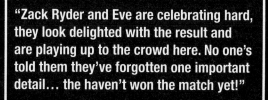

"Zack Ryder and Eve are celebrating hard, they look delighted with the result and are playing up to the crowd here. No one's told them they've forgotten one important detail… the haven't won the match yet!"

"Oh no! The Miz is up and has caught Ryder. He's landed it, and it's a nasty. A Skull-Crushing Finale and it looks like it's lights out for Zack!"

75

"The ref's counted it and the result is in the books. It's a win for Team Johnny thanks to The Miz pinning Zack Ryder. No one in the crowd can believe it, least of Ryder's main squeeze, Eve!"

"This is a huge victory for Laurinaitis and the W means he's now in charge of both Raw and SmackDown! What will this mean for Teddy Long and his team of Superstars?"

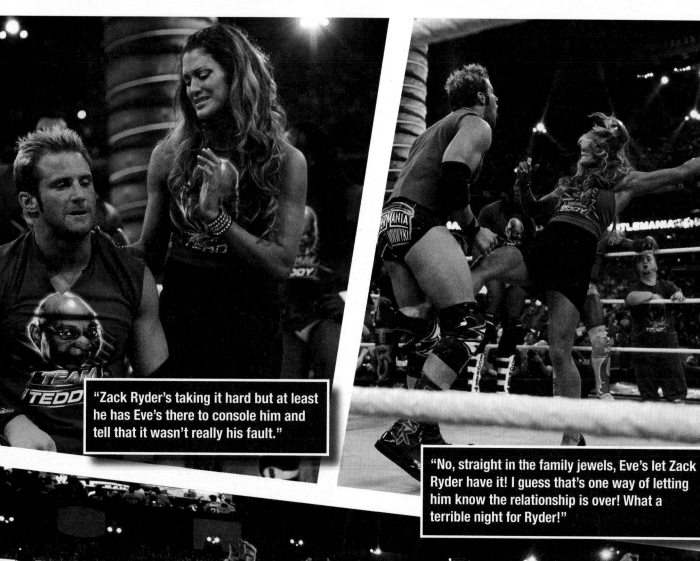

"Zack Ryder's taking it hard but at least he has Eve's there to console him and tell that it wasn't really his fault."

"No, straight in the family jewels, Eve's let Zack Ryder have it! I guess that's one way of letting him know the relationship is over! What a terrible night for Ryder!"

"They might not have deserved it, but they were smart enough to get the victory. And it's one that will have huge repercussions, not only for Teddy Long and his team, but also every Superstar in the WWE!"

# The Finishers

All WWE Superstars have moves they rely on to finish their matches. Undertaker puts people away with a well-timed Tombstone, Shawn Michaels used Sweet Chin Music to devastating effect, while legend Macho Man Randy Savage ended hundreds of matches with his diving elbow drop.

Some of the current WWE crop have taken the finishers to the next level. Take a look at seven of the best.

## 619

### Rey Mysterio – 619 & West Coast Pop

The masked man has earned a reputation all over the world for his high-flying expertise. Nowhere in the ring is safe with Rey around! His two-part finishing move is among the best ever seen. First, he swings through the ropes to deliver two feet to his opponent's face before climbing to the top rope catching two feet around his foe's ears, backflipping and slamming to the mat for the one, two, three. Wow!

# Attitude Adjustment

## John Cena – Attitude Adjustment

The perfect blend of brute strength and perfect technique, the Attitude Adjustment has been winning matches for John Cena for years. After softening up his rival, Cena grabs them and lifts them on his shoulders. In one fluid movement, Cena flips them on to the canvas, ties them up for the three-count and picks up another victory!

# Pedigree

## Triple H – Pedigree

With his in-ring toughness and experience, Triple H is already more than a match for most Superstars. Throw in the Pedigree though and it's easy to see why Triple H has captured the gold so many times. An adapted piledriver, the Pedigree sees Triple H trap his opponent's head between, grab both their arms and drive their head into the mat. Game over!

# RKO

## Randy Orton – RKO

Wanna know what Triple H, Sheamus and Ric Flair all have in common? They've all been finished by Randy Orton's RKO! A lightning fast, adapted neck breaker drop, Orton can land the RKO at any moment meaning his opponents are in danger from the moment they step through the ropes!

# Rock Bottom

## The Rock – Rock Bottom

Just like the Rock himself, Rock Bottom is bombastic, powerful and completely deadly. Quick as a flash, Rock tucks his head under his opponents arm, lifts them high above the ring and then drives them straight back into the canvas. With nothing free to break their fall, and the Rock's weight crushing down on top of them, it's easy to predict what happens next!

# Tombstone Piledriver

## Undertaker – Tombstone Piledriver

Arguably the most famous finisher in the business, the Deadman's Tombstone has said 'goodnight' to all who have been unlucky enough be caught in it. Undertaker grabs his foe, puts their head between his legs before upending them and dropping them straight onto their craniums. More often than not, a swift 'One two three' from the referee swiftly follows!

# Sweet Chin music

## Shawn Michaels – Sweet Chin Music

The list of Superstars who have been put to sleep by Sweet Chin Music over the years reads like a Who's Who of modern sports Entertainment! During his career, HBK's fast right boot won him titles, respect, revenge and got him out of more than his fair share of trouble. And no matter how bad his opponents beat him down, Sweet Chin Music was ready to played at any time!

# Tale Of The Tape:
# UNDERTAKER
## Match Profile

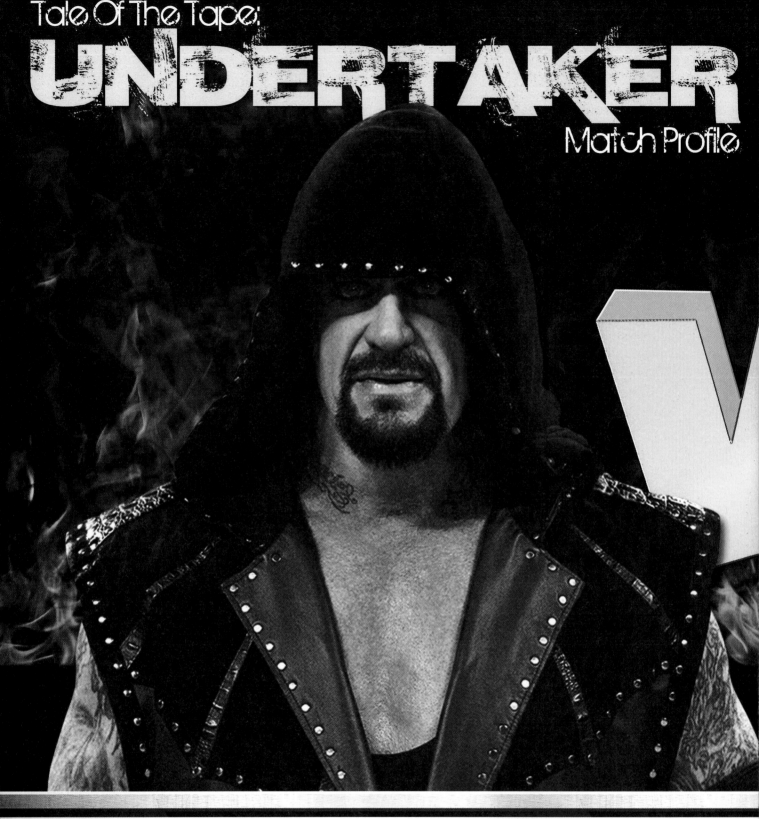

**HEIGHT:** 6'10"
**WEIGHT:** 299 LBS
**FROM:** DEATH VALLEY
**SIGNATURE MOVE:** CHOKESLAM, TOMBSTONE, LAST RIDE
**CAREER HIGHLIGHTS:** WWE CHAMPION, WORLD HEAVYWEIGHT CHAMPION, WORLD TAG TEAM CHAMPION, WCW TAG TEAM CHAMPION, HARDCORE CHAMPION, UNDEFEATED AT WRESTLEMANIA (20-0)

## Did you know?

- Undertaker is one of WWE's longest-serving Superstars. He first made his debut with the company in 1990 as a mystery contestant in The Million Dollar Man Ted Dibiase's team at *Survivor Series*.

- As well as producing dominant performances against almost everyone he has faced in the ring, Undertaker has also been a pioneer of many matches during his career. He was the first Superstar to win a Casket Match in 1992, the first Buried Alive in 1996 and competed in the inaugural Hell In A Cell Match in October 1997.

- While Undertaker calls Death Valley his home, he could easily argue that it should be *WrestleMania*. In 20 appearances at the event, he has won every time.

# Tale Of The Tape:
# TRIPLE H
## Match Profile

**HEIGHT:** 6'4"
**WEIGHT:** 255 LBS
**FROM:** GREENWICH, CONNECTICUT
**SIGNATURE MOVE:** PEDIGREE
**CAREER HIGHLIGHTS:**
WWE CHAMPION,
WORLD HEAVYWEIGHT CHAMPION,
INTERCONTINENTAL CHAMPION,
UNIFIED WWE TAG TEAM CHAMPION,
WORLD TAG TEAM CHAMPION,
EUROPEAN CHAMPION, 1997 KING
OF THE RING, 2002 ROYAL
RUMBLE MATCH WINNER

## Did you know?

○ Triple H holds the record for the most reigns as World Champ in the WWE. Over his career he's held the WWE and World Heavyweight Championship 13 times combined!

○ You have to go all the way back to 1995 to see Triple H's first appearance in WWE. Back then he was known only by his full name, Hunter Hearst Helmsley, the Connecticut Blueblood!

○ Wanna get a physique like Triple H's? He shows you how you can in his book, Making the Game: Triple H's Approach to a Better Body.

○ As well as being a legendary competitor, Triple H is also the company's Chief Operating Officer. After a recent legal run-in with Brock Lesnar about his return to the WWE, the pair got physical with Lesnar breaking Triple H's

"What a match we have coming up! But before the competitors come to the ring, welcome tonight's special guest referee. It's WWE legend Shawn Michaels, the Heartbreak Kid!"

"The Showstopper is back! Michaels looks like he's loving every second of being back in front of the *WrestleMania* crowd. But he's got a job to do tonight, he's the third man in the ring with two of the most dangerous Superstars in WWE history!"

"And here comes the first one now! Triple H looks mean, moody and fired up for tonight's fight! What an entrance."

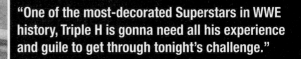

"The crowd is going nuts but there's no time for Triple H to enjoy their applause, he knows the challenge that awaits him in the cage tonight!"

"One of the most-decorated Superstars in WWE history, Triple H is gonna need all his experience and guile to get through tonight's challenge."

"Triple was called a 'coward who lives in Shawn Michaels' shadow' in the build-up to this match. He certainly doesn't look like that now!"

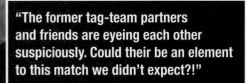

"The former tag-team partners and friends are eyeing each other suspiciously. Could their be an element to this match we didn't expect?!"

"Woah! Here comes the Deadman. I wouldn't wanna be in Triple H's boots this evening, Undertaker looks terrifying!"

"Undertaker is putting his incredible WrestleMania® record on the line again tonight. He's appeared at 19 events prior to this night and is undefeated. Will he make it 20 wins or is tonight the night his 0 has to go?!"

"He's finally made his way to the ring. In the entire walk to the ring, Undertaker hasn't taken his eyes off Triple H once."

"We're seconds away from hearing the bell and this incredible match getting under way. Only one thing remains, the steel cell is being lowered slowly around the ring. The *WrestleMania* crowd here knows something special is about to take place here tonight in Miami!"

"Undertaker connects with a huge clothesline that almost knocks Triple H right out of his boots!"

"Wait a second, what is this? It looks like the Deadman is setting Triple H up for a Tombstone. Surely, it's too early in the match to land one of them?"

"He's gonna get it! This could end early for Triple H, no one kicks out of a pin after Undertaker lands his signature move."

"I don't believe Triple H kicked out! But his troubles are far from over, Undertaker is using the top rope to land an enormous leg drop!"

"Michaels goes for the count. After the punishment that has been handed out to Triple H tonight there is surely no way he can turn this around now? One, two…"

"He kicked out! And now it's time for Triple H to start landing some hurt bombs! There's a foreign object in the ring – H landed some strikes with a sledgehammer. But wait, was the Deadman playing possum? Triple H has fallen straight into a triangle choke."

"Someone's going for a ride! The steel steps are now in the ring and, standing on top of them, Undertaker has thrown Triple H 10 foot into the air!"

"He's going for the cover! The crowd counts along with HBK. 'One, two, three!'"

"Incredible! Undertaker has done it – he's extended his unbelievable WrestleMania® record again. He's now undefeated in 20 appearances at sports entertainment's biggest show. Surely a record that will never be beaten!"

"Triple H played his part tonight and Michaels knows it. He fought with inredible bravery and only just came up short."

"What a show of class. Shawn Michaels and Undertaker are helping Triple H back to the locker room! A perfect display of sportsmanship to end one of the most incredible nights in WWE history!"

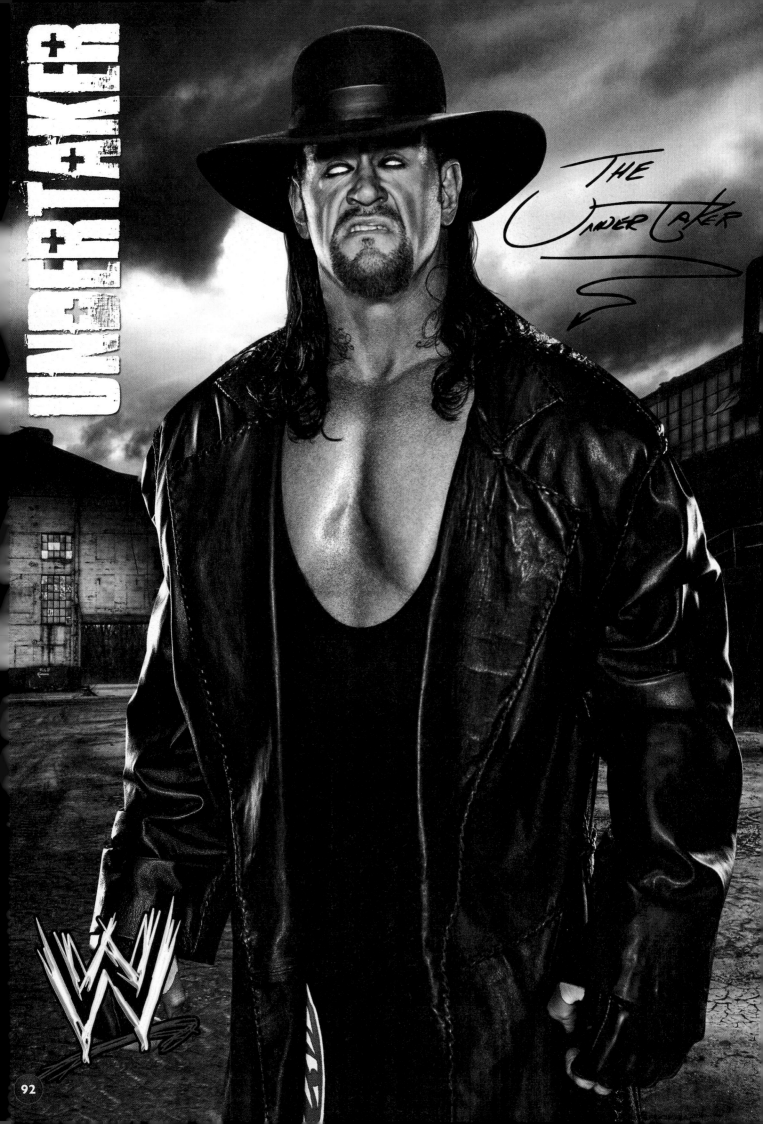

UNDERTAKER

The Undertaker

TRIPLE H

# Answers

**P26-27 The Heavyweight WWE Quiz Part One –
Hall Of Fame**
1. B
2. A
3. C
4. C
5. A
6. B
7. A
8. C
9. B
10. C

**P40 WWE Spot The Difference**

**P41 Name That Superstar**
1. KOFI KINGSTON
2. HEATH SLATER
3. JINDER MAHAL
4. JUSTIN GABRIEL
5. TENSAI

6. R-TRUTH
7. SHEAMUS
8. ZACK RYDER
9. GREAT KHALI

**P54 WWE Wordsearch**

| T | R | I | P | L | E | H |   | W | R | Y | D | E | R | F | G |
|---|---|---|---|---|---|---|---|---|---|---|---|---|---|---|---|
| R | A | A | H | K | E | W | V | S | G | Q | R | E | F | H |
| U | N | D | E | R | T | A | K | E | R | D | E | D | G | E |
| E | D | F | C | E | N | A | E | E | V | A | P | A | C | A |
| W | Y | S | O | B | Q | C | B | A | A | K | I | N | L | R |
| Q | O | X | B | D | W | J | G | L | N | C | I | Q | T |
| L | R | E | Y | M | Y | S | T | E | R | I | O | E | L | B |
| T | T | D | R | W | V | X | G | N | B | F | G | L | Q |
| R | O | I | H | U | N | I | C | O | T | Z | D | H | E |
| E | N | B | O | U | D | S | W | V | S | H | K | R | B | A |
| K | R | D | D | P | S | H | E | A | M | U | S | Y | K | K |
| O | Q | D | E | A | V | N | G | S | E | G | A | A | V | K |
| O | K | D | S | V | A | H | I | O | S | W | V | N | R | I |
| B | R | O | C | K | L | E | S | N | A | R | V | D | B | D |
| Y | I | H | O | R | N | S | W | O | G | G | L | E | R | L |

**P55 Colossal Crossword**

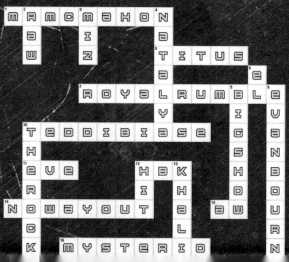